FORMULA 4 SUCCESS

4 SIMPLE STEPS TO ACHIEVE ANYTHING YOU WANT IN LIFE

GERALD DUBOSE

All rights reserved. No part of this publication may be reproduced, distributed or transmitted in any form or by any means, including photocopying, recording, or other electronic or mechanical methods, without the prior written permission of the publisher, except in the case of brief quotations embodied in critical reviews and certain other noncommercial uses permitted by copyright law. For permission requests, write to the publisher at the address below:

Gerald DuBose

www.thenewwealthorder.com/contact

Copyright © 2017 Gerald DuBose

All rights reserved.

ISBN: 0692701389

ISBN-13: **978-0692701386**

DEDICATION

God thank you for the gift of life

For the love that you have given me

For the gifts and talents

For the challenges and blessings

For the lessons and successes

I am eternally grateful

Father I thank you

TABLE OF CONTENTS

Before Words	x
Introduction	xii
Chapter One	2
Chapter Two	28
Chapter Three	64
Chapter Four	90
Chapter Five	101
Chapter Six	108
Chapter Seven	116
Chapter Eight	125
Chapter Nine	134
Acknowledgements	142
Resources	143
About The Author	145

YOU ARE A SUCCESS

BEFORE WORDS

Imagine a life of ultimate freedom. A life where you are capable of creating whatever you want. As a matter of fact, in this world you have the superpower of creation and understanding. You are one of the most powerful super beings on the planet.

Your powers are legendary many want to know you. Some envy your capabilities and mock your shortcomings. Though with your indomitable will and the love from those that love you, you're so strong the mockery bounces off you like blanks from a starter pistol. What would you do with such power? What would you create? We are about to find out together.

Welcome to The Formula 4 Success

YOU ARE A SUCCESS

INTRODUCTION

In this journey we have called life we are in a constant pursuit. There is a well-known quote by Thomas Jefferson that says "We hold these truths to be self-evident: that all men are created equal; that they are endowed by their Creator with certain unalienable rights; that among these are life, liberty, and the pursuit of happiness."

One of our main objectives in life is to achieve. We are on a consistent uphill trek to find the success we would like on several levels everyday including: happiness, love, career etc. There seems to be an ongoing search for that destination called success but what are we using as a barometer to measure that very thing?

Being a business cultivator one of the first things we do is check the metrics. How is said company performing in these certain key areas? We take those figures check them against different variables to assess the status of the company. From there we can develop a plan of action moving forward to help the company be more successful. Now let's flip that question how frequently do any of us do the very same thing with our lives?

This book is my little epitaph to the exploration of success. The beliefs, values and understandings thereof. What are we chasing and why are we chasing it? It is a birds-eye view of success in its purest form.

I do not claim to be an expert however I've come up with some simple concepts and constructs that have worked for me and found them to be universally true for the highest achievers of our society.

Let's move forward in the journey together. It is my sincerest hope that The Formula 4 Success sparks a new internal inferno, gives you the power to increase your life to its fullest capacity and achieve success on levels unbound!

PART I
Success Beliefs and Map

YOU ARE A SUCCESS

CHAPTER ONE

OUTLINING SUCCESS

"Always bear in mind that your own resolution to succeed is more important than any other." -
Abraham Lincoln

Success is a word that is often thrown around freely. As if it's an abstract concept that we are always chasing but never obtain. Success, happiness, wealthy, rich, poor are all words that the average human being struggles with trying to be or not to be because of the emotional experiences that we believe they create.

If we are looking at our experiences through the eyes of others we will quantify all of those words by: the clothes we wear, career path chosen hierarchal titles, what type of car we drive, how large or small the house we live in, how frequently we vacation etc. In other words, (no pun intended) typically, these words are viewed as a means of classifying one's status.

According to societal views if you are successful you:

- Drive a certain type of car
- You live in a large home in some exclusive community.
- You eat at the finest restaurants
- Your kids go the best private schools

The world is at your fingertips, right? For the most part we all know that this isn't quite the truth though. As with any emotional adjective that we use to describe our experiences in life, success is subjective. It is only in accordance with our own rules, definition, tasks and completion thereof that success can be achieved.

Now I suppose that you are asking what does this mean for me? For the person reading these words what this means is that throughout the next few pages we are going to examine what that construct looks like for you. How you have been viewing success in the past. We will then assist you in building an outline for success that is applicable to your present life and your brightest future.

Outlining Your Path to success

In this phase, we will take a look at what has brought you to this point in your life. Every journey has a starting point and a destination. Dealing with what has shaped your past and current situation will serve as your launching point to the great successes of your future.

As is with everything that you would like to improve upon you must first know where you are to improve or progress.

When doing the following exercise, it is extremely imperative that you be brutally honest and not ask for help during the process. This is your journey and no one else's. There are a couple work pages that follow the exercise or if you choose you can use a separate piece of paper. Take your time to answer each question with <u>at least three beliefs</u>. The purpose is to get out complete thoughts and what's in your heart. For example:

1. What is success?

Success is having one million dollars in the bank.

Success is doing whatever I want.

Success is owning a mansion.

Now it's your turn to do so. If at all possible it would be best to do the exercise in a quiet environment. This exercise is about going deep into what beliefs you have about how success appears in your life. It is more difficult to do if you are having to pay attention to other things during this process.

Give yourself space and time to do the work. This is not a race to get done quickly. It is an exploration of your emotions and beliefs which is never easy. Remember the process only works to the extent that you work the process.

Success Belief Exercise

1. What is success? (Define it)

2. What does success look like? (Describe it)

3. How do you feel about successful people?

4. What are the differences between successful people and unsuccessful people?

5. What do you feel has kept you from the success that you would like?

FORMULA 4 SUCCESS

FORMULA 4 SUCCESS

Ok you are done with the beliefs exercise. Let's take a moment to reflect on it. I want you to go back through the list to look at your answers and see where they stem from. Often the feelings we associate with things or experiences are not our own. We learn to associate meanings with words we heard as children from people that we look up to and then we carry that around with us for so long that we began to accept the thoughts as our own.

I know that as a child one thing I heard a lot was that if you want to be successful you have to go to college so that you can get a "good" education. It was spoken to me repeatedly by teachers, assistant principals and some of those I love. I also heard that you can do anything you really set your mind to regardless of what other people tell you. Now these aren't polar opposites on the surface, but what if you have set in your mind that you want to create something that has never existed then how does that play into the standard "good" education piece? Even in my youthful mind those two didn't connect properly.

It is true in order to go beyond a standard we must know and understand what that standard is. Did that have to come from 'formal' education? Did that mean I should have a MBA, MA or MS in something to truly understand it?

In my little brain, all of that sounded like I was being sold on getting a MBS. A Masters in BS!!!

Please don't misinterpret what I am conveying here. Education is paramount in achieving what we want however the "good" part is immensely subjective. The information that is necessary for you to achieve what you want in your life may be vastly different than the information I need to achieve what I want in my life. There are certain truthful nuances that will be universally applicable across the achievement spectrum but the process of learning the information we need to create what it is we are meant to create will be different.

I to this day have no formal degree from any accredited university. I have no fancy letters to put after my name. I however have guided my own companies to high levels of success in various industries. I have and still do advise C- level executives on how to best move their businesses forward. I help them to increase their productivity and profitability. These achievements didn't come from accepting someone else's beliefs on success as my own but instead disassociating myself from what others felt was right then forging onward with what I knew was right for me.

Accepted beliefs are one of the biggest blocks on our path to success. It is imperative to understand what are beliefs that were given to us, what thoughts are our own and what beliefs serve us in achieving success.

Disassociation Exercise

We will leave you a couple pages here to be able to go back through the questions, of the Success Belief exercise mark each belief with the name of the person that you got this belief from and underline their name. For example, if what you wrote was a belief or feeling that came from something you heard from your mother put your mother's name beside it or a brother put your brother's name there. Do that for each belief that you wrote down in response to the questions asked.

Your new answers may look something like this:

Success is having one million dollars in the bank. - *Uncle John*

Success is doing whatever I want. - *Mrs. Thompson 6th grade teacher*

Important to note that you don't have to show this list to anyone else.

This process is for understanding in your life. Sometimes you have to dig up the root of something in order to decide whether you need to remove, replant or replace it for your harvest to flourish. We will delve deeper into this concept of remove, replant, replace in the next chapter.

Over the next few pages let's explore what some of the roots are.

Success Belief Exercise
(Disassociation)

1. What is success? (Define it)

2. What does success look like? (Describe it)

3. How do you feel about successful people?

4. What are the differences between successful people and unsuccessful people?

5. What do you feel has kept you from the success that you would like?

FORMULA 4 SUCCESS

FORMULA 4 SUCCESS

You have now looked at not only what opinions and views have shaped your thinking about success but also where those thoughts come from. Did you find that most of the beliefs you had written in the exercise were not even your own? Did you notice any patterns in the beliefs?

In our youth people who love and care about us give us **their beliefs** to try to protect us. They want nothing more than to keep us safe from harm. To keep us focused trying to ensure that we live not only a good life but one that exceeds their own.

There is an inherent need for every generation to see progress through its progeny. It is natural for the middle-aged as well the elderly to pass on what they feel are life lessons to the young.

However, the challenge is we all have individual lessons that we must learn. Thought processes that we have to nurture for that very progress to happen. You are given your own set of unique challenges to go through to become what you must so that you can contribute to society in a meaningful manner.

The exercises that you have done in this first chapter are really exercises in clarity. It is intended so that you can without question gain insight into what and who is shaping your beliefs and emotions around success.

The disassociation exercise in particular allows us to see whose beliefs are firmly rooted in our reality today.

Let's go into a review of chapter one to get a gauge for where we are.

Quick review of what we have done so far:

-**Success Beliefs** What your views are around success

-**Disassociation Exercise** Where do your beliefs around success come from

We are not only clear on what some of the challenges are but what the root of them are. Which has effectively allowed us to become empowered to

FORMULA 4 SUCCESS

create a better future. In the next chapter, we will begin to lay the ground work to building our success.

CHAPTER TWO

REMOVE REPLANT REPLACE

"Sometimes you have to dig up the root of something in order to decide whether you need to replant, replace or remove it for your harvest to flourish"- **Gerald DuBose**

Everything that is good to you is not good for you. An old idiom I have heard for quite some time. Kind of makes me feel old even saying "quite some time" but I digress. The adage "Everything that is good to you is not good for you" has merit though.

There are a lot of things we do consistently, even more things that we hold on to because of the sentimental value that we placed on them.

This emotional attachment to things and thoughts can affect our relationships, career, finances, success and happiness. Emotion is the catalyst of life. It is the very energy that drives most human behavior. It inhibits or enhances our ability to perform.

All the beliefs from the disassociation exercise are exactly what is creating your emotions which are effecting the level of success you are achieving.

Our brains and hearts are like farmland; they are fertile soil for us to cultivate the seeds of promise that have been given to us as at birth. What you plant in your gardens will dictate your ability to learn, grow, expand and succeed in our lifetime.

REMOVE REPLANT REPLACE

There was a story of a farmer who inherited his family's farm after his father passed. He loved the farm. His family had the farm for over three generations. It was now his turn to do what was necessary to keep the family business going. For three generations, the family had a very moderate and honest business selling apples. Six months after his father passed the orders for the apples began to dry up.

The young farmer had long wanted to plant oranges on the farm the problem was he knew it was no way the rest of the family would approve of such a decision because there was nowhere to plant orange trees every inch of the farm was consumed by the apple trees.

This caused the farmer much turmoil because the apples were not selling like they used to and he had no room to plant the oranges he so desperately wanted. After six more months, the troubles had quadrupled. the farm had now gone into foreclosure status. The family business was going down the tubes, the business loan was in default on top of him falling into a deep depression.

How many times has this been your situation? How many times have you been just like the farmer? How many times have you looked at that old apple tree when you were thinking about that orange tree you knew could possibly change your life but you couldn't bear the thought of replacing the apple trees because someone you love and respect told you that those trees needed to be there?

Perhaps they did at that point in time but is it bearing the fruit now that is necessary for your harvest. Is that belief that worked so good for you at 15 still serving you well now at 25, 35, 45, 55? It is so utterly important for us to examine those things in our farmland (our hearts, our brains) to evaluate everything that you have planted. So you can ask is this going to serve me in succeeding at what I am looking to accomplish?

Even more so will what is planted reap the harvest that you need or want in your life?

Remove

All too often we see people that clutter their houses with things that no longer have use or even worse things they have never used. They are compulsive buyers always feeling the need to get something until they eventually run out of room. In most situations, we call these people hoarders.

Many of us often do the same thing psychologically and emotionally. We hoard many feelings, beliefs, facts, thought processes that are outdated, no longer of use yet in still we allow them to be pervasive in our decisions about life. These old thoughts and feelings stifle our ability to move forward with confidence as well as inhibit our growth.

There are just somethings that are useless to us in our journey at this point. These thoughts/feelings/habits must be removed for the betterment of your life. It's perfectly fine to clear space for more empowering better beliefs.

Removal Exercise

Let's put this into action right now. I would like you to think about and write out at least three negative beliefs you may have about: yourself, relationships, money and happiness right now. After you write them out I want you to smile and look at them for at least one minute really get a feel for the power in the words. Now stand and with force say this declaration:

I ___(insert your name)_____ from this moment forth will not allow these tattered detrimental thoughts to be part of my existence. I thank you for sharing but I release you. We are free together. I am better.

Now scratch out the 1st thought on your list. Do the declaration again then scratch the 2nd off your list. Repeat the process until you have reached the end of each list.

I have left some space on the following pages for you to be able to do your work. As always be honest, take your time and trust the process. If possible don't do the exercise in one sitting. Write out your thoughts and give yourself 24 hours to come back and revisit them to ensure that these are the things that you feel in your heart of hearts that must be removed. We are about to dig up and remove some blocks from the roots!

SELF

1.

2.

3.

REMOVE REPLANT REPLACE

RELATIONSHIPS

1.

2.

3.

MONEY

1.

2.

3.

HAPPINESS

1.

2.

3.

Great job on completing the exercise! Were you able to uncover and pull up some deeply rooted blocks to clear the way for new and better things for your future? Removing is the first part of this process let us now go to the second phase.

REPLANT

Certain times in our lives we omit or forget about key points of lessons allowing them to fall by the wayside. Our farmlands (brains and hearts) are all filled with several malnourished understandings, thoughts, feelings or beliefs. Which ultimately in the end, could have tremendous influence on the abundance of the harvest we reap in our lifetime.

In the continual quest for growth we may find it necessary to assess the things we have heard, written or seen and view them with a fresh perspective (fertile soil). From a fresh perspective, we can then view some overlooked past information and be able to utilize it much better at this current juncture of life.

For example: My father used to tell me frequently in my adolescence that I need to understand 'education, exploration and utilization are the gateway to destiny' Like most children I just thought that he was talking in riddles to try to sound profound. I felt like he wanted me to be astounded by the statement because at that time I had absolutely no clue what in the world my father was talking about!!!

So, like most kids I continued on with my life believing that I knew better than him and his fancy word phrasing wasn't going to phase me. Because he couldn't understand what it's like for me growing up in this time. How could he know what he was talking about he was old? Even though he was my best friend in the world, I didn't feel like he understood the world I was growing up in.

My father last told me that when I was 20 years old. I still didn't quite get what he was trying to tell me. He made his transition from this life that same year. Even at his most ill he was still trying to look out for his baby boy imparting some wise wine to nourish my very soul 'education, exploration and utilization are the gateway to destiny.'

It took me: 40 years, thousands of bad decisions, innumerable mistakes, countless books, tapes, videos, cd's, workshops and endless sleepless nights to get it. I had been listening to the words but I wasn't hearing what he was saying.

My brain had not been through enough training. My mental muscles weren't strong enough to get it. The soil was fertile but not yet cultivated enough for the seeds of that wisdom to grow and blossom.

I came back to the idea last year and replanted it in the fertile cultivated soil and already some of its fruit is feeding people. This book is just one example of its fruits.

What are some things you have heard that perhaps you weren't quite able to understand? Something that perhaps you discounted as rhetoric or nonsense at the time because it just didn't seem very tangible? What is something that was way too honest the moment you heard it but now is totally applicable in your life?

If you are anything like most people including myself, I'm sure that you can think of quite a few over sights you have had on taking in 'wise wine'.

What is wise wine? Wise Wine is informative beneficial takeaways that you get from conversations or experiences you have. Some people call it knowledge nuggets, some say gleaning gold. I call it wise wine because red wine is nourishment for your body, in the same vein when I gain insight or knowledge from an interaction I call it wise wine since the information is nourishment for my life.

To make all this talk applicable here is your next exercise. As always take your time as you do the processes.

Replant Exercise

1. List 3 empowering thoughts that you have heard about yourself that are applicable to your life now but you were dismissive of when you initially heard them

2. List 3 empowering thoughts that you have heard about relationships that are applicable

to your life now but you were dismissive of when you initially heard them

3. List 3 empowering thoughts that you have heard about money that are applicable to your life now but you were dismissive of when you initially heard them

4. List 3 empowering thoughts that you have heard about happiness that are applicable to your life now but you were dismissive of when you initially heard them

REMOVE REPLANT REPLACE

SELF

1.

2.

3.

RELATIONSHIPS

1.

2.

3.

REMOVE REPLANT REPLACE

MONEY

1.

2.

3.

HAPPINESS

1.

2.

3.

Phenomenal job! Viewing things that we may have overlooked or didn't get but can understand now is so vital to our growth. Replanting can perhaps be looked at as the maturation part of the process. On to the third and final phase.

Replace

Do you remember the story of the farmer from the very beginning of this chapter? Holding on to outdated thoughts/beliefs allowing them to take up space that new ideas and beliefs could be occupying, can harm or even kill your harvest. What worked yesterday was great yesterday however, every day we are presented a new set of challenges and what was yesterday's best practices quickly become today's dinosaurs.

Einstein once said "We cannot solve our problems with the same thinking we used when we created them." Far too many of us utilize yesterday's beliefs, thoughts, ideals, and emotions in trying to create our future. It's nearly impossible for that to work especially when most of what's being utilized is disempowering or irrelevant beliefs, thoughts, ideals from many years ago that created the current issues.

Wishing for change doesn't work. Praying for change doesn't work. Hoping for change doesn't work. For the life, you live to change you must **create** the change. Old beliefs and habits must be replaced by new beliefs and habits that fit the change we are seeking. If you want success you must be willing to modify your behavior to fit the person you are becoming not the person you were even 10 minutes ago before you read these words.

How much of the person that *you are right now*, you are willing to let go of, is in direct proportion to how much of the person that *you want to become* will succeed.

I'm certain that we can all think of an activity, a food, a movie, a song or heck even a person that we were totally in love with 10 years back. Now looking back, you have no understanding of what or why we thought we loved that activity, food, movie, person or song because where you are now you would never do that thing or see that person. That food doesn't quite have the same taste it did when you were liking it so much. What has changed? Surely you are the same person you were back then, right?

Of course not. You have grown, life has a new feel to it now than it did then. The music, the activities, the movies, the people have changed a lot in the last 10 years because *why* you like what you like has changed as well as who you are.

Most times the choices in life are made on auto-pilot. As much as we like to think we are *'consciously'* choosing, we are being guided by cognitive shortcuts. To allow your brain the ability to carry on with protecting you in addition to handling your bodily functions.

Here's a hard truth, your brain's primary function is not to ensure that you are successful. There are thousands of bits of information being disseminated every second by your brain, which begs to reason why we would believe its focusing on our success naturally. A vast majority of our decisions aren't decisions at all they are quick neurological responses to past situations.

Joseph Roux said it this way "Reason guides but a small part of man and that the least interesting. The rest obeys feeling true or false and passion good or bad."

In essence your feelings contribute much more to your actions than your intellect. Which means the better we understand what we feel and why we feel what we feel. The more control we have over our decisions. More control we have over our decisions means more control of our actions.

What feelings are you having that used to work for you but may be holding you back? How impassioned are you by those feelings? What can you replace those feelings with that serve you now?

In the following exercise, you will take a sojourn into the depths of those feelings to create a new present.

Replace Exercise

1. Write out at least five and up to nine feelings you have about your life that you have accepted simply as this is how I am. These are your <u>present day</u> defining statements. For example:

   I feel that being successful takes a lot of hard work.

2. Give each feeling an impassioned rating from 1-10. 1-very weak passion 10-extreme passion

3. Rewrite any of your present-day statements that rate 7 and below to make them more impassioned. We will replace the present with more empowering views. These will become your <u>future defining statements</u>.

Present Day Statements

Present Day Statements

Impassioned Ratings

Future Defining Statements

You have done a great deal of work in this chapter. Let's do a quick review of the progress made from this chapter.

In this chapter, we were able to accomplish:

-**Removing** some negative beliefs that have cluttered our farmland

-**Replanting** malnourished, vital overlooked ideas and concepts

-**Replacing** weak less empowered feelings with empowered feelings that serve your success

In the next chapter, we will create a MAP to start heading toward our destination of success.

CHAPTER THREE

CREATING YOUR MAP

"The leader of the past was a person who knew how to tell. The leader of the future will be a person who knows how to ask."- **Peter Drucker**

When you decide to go to a place the first thing you need is an address. Doesn't matter where it is in the world if you don't have an address you cannot get to that specific location without a specific address.

How come we don't use the same thinking in planning where we want our life to go? When we do our life planning, we tend to be very general in choosing what we want and where we want to go in life. There is little wonder then why it's challenging to accomplish the goals that we set for ourselves. Without specificity, we can't get to our destination because we have no direction.

I grew up in Washington DC my father drove a cab at night. He knew every inch of the city. He could tell you what neighborhoods to visit depending on the experience you wanted to have. Maybe even more importantly what neighborhoods to stay away from if safety was high on your priority list. If you hopped in my father's car and didn't know where you wanted to go, he would immediately put you out.

I believe that life treats you much the same in that regard. If you have no certain destination, then life leaves you where you are until you figure out where the heck you are going.

These life decisions are daunting for most of us. Usually the first thing about 75% of people that you ask what they want, their first response is I don't know?!?!?! This is especially vexing because how can you obtain what you are after, have a clear vision or develop a strategy if you don't know what you are going after?

Yet this is the space a large proportion of society operates from. They come from the thinking of 'I don't know what I want but I d on't want ____ and something has to change.' Does that statement sound familiar to you? If it does, then you are not alone. A large portion of society has said this statement including myself at one point in my life. So how do we change it? How do we bring things into focus and make some choices that will positively impact our lives today? We begin by creating a map. We start with what.

WHAT DO YOU DESIRE

Simon Sinek has popularized the phrase "Start with Why" in his book by the same title. I say that if you want to get to that next level of achievement or fulfillment we must start with what. Why seems to always leads back to what. So back to the question what do you really want?

Looking at four key areas we will establish what you truly want.

Life Desire Exercise

1. Write down three things you really want for yourself. These are things that you feel would bring you immense joy. These are things just for you.

2. Write down three things you really want for your career. These must be things that bring you ultimate fulfillment.

3. Write down three things you really want for your spiritual life. These are things that bring you peace, comfort and confidence.

4. Write down three things you really want in your relationships. These must be things that make you feel loved and connected to those you love/care for.

Self

Career

Spirit

Relationships

You have established a basis to work from, on what it is you want *now* to bring it in perfect focus. Time to turn it into a vision. A vision so clear to you that you can see it, feel it and almost touch it.

A major hang-up for people is the ability to focus. If it is in your line of sight or heavy on your heart suddenly whatever it is becomes a lot easier to focus on. When something isn't in that line of sight or heavy on our hearts most of us don't have the situational awareness to stay cognizant of that thing.

This is the reason why vision is so important. The clearer your aspirations the easier it is to focus on them. If you don't have a vision all you have is a dream. I am not saying that having dreams aren't good, however, if you never take time to turn that dream into a vision your dreams usually are soon forgotten.

Think about this, can you remember what you dreamt two nights ago? Chances are you can't unless something traumatic or shocking happened in that dream. Dreams are too vague too cloudy, that is partly the reason why they are easily forgotten.

The difference between a dreamer and a visionary is the dreamer is usually content with having the dream. While a visionary turns their dream into reality. Everybody has dreams but visionaries change the world!

We will take your work from the life desire exercise and crystalize it so that the vision is clear and we can begin creating our destinations.

CRYSTALIZATON EXERCISE

1. Copy your answers from the all the categories of the Life Desires Exercises to their corresponding categories on the following pages. Give each desire a rank of 1-10 in importance to you

2. Eliminate the lowest importance in each section.

3. If there are any two that rank of same importance in their category asses them by which you'd rather have first. Repeat the process until there is only one answer in each category.

Self

Career

Spirit

Relationships

Since you now have what you want clearly in focus. How does it feel to have vision into your future? I would venture to say probably feels pretty good maybe even powerful.

Next we will move into the second phase of your map.

Creating the Timeline

Creating a clear vision for yourself is crucial to your success. Understanding when things need to be done is just as critical to your mission. Time is important to setting yourself on the right course. Time makes things specific. We talked a lot about specifics earlier in the chapter, we have to know when a task must be completed.

The luxury of time is immutable. We can only change our usage of time. One thing you can do to better manage time is to do what we just did in the previous exercise that is prioritize properly. The creation of a timeline brings perspective that can allow us to truly see our way to success.

Timeline Exercise

1. On the following pages write out your 30, 90, 180, 365 destinations from the four prioritized desires.

   Example

   Self

   Priority Desire: Losing 20lbs

   30 days- lose 5lbs

   90 days- lose 15lbs

   180 days- lose 20lbs

Self

Prioritized Desire:

30 days-

90 days-

180 days -

365 days-

Career

Prioritized Desire:

30 days-

90 days-

180 days -

365 days-

Spirit

Prioritized Desire:

30 days-

90 days-

180 days -

365 days-

Relationships

Prioritized Desire:

30 days-

90 days-

180 days -

365 days-

The timeline is completed and most of our map is done. All we need to do is take our timeline with each Desire, incorporate the Formula with each and our MAP is complete. Now we can begin to assimilate the Formula 4 Success to complete the MAP.

Before we jump into the Formula we should do a quick review of what we have done in this chapter:

-**Life Desires** What you truly want in your life

-**Crystallization** Prioritize our life desires

-**Create the Timeline** Make the priorities tangible

PART II
THE FORMULA

CHAPTER FOUR

RIGHT ACTIONS

*"The only thing you own in life is your actions!"- **Gerald DuBose***

In the movie, *I, Robot*, Will Smith plays a police detective named Del Spooner that is living in the age of robotics. Challenge is Spooner distrust robots due to an accident he was in and the robot calculated it was best to save his life over that of a 12-yr old girl because his survival probability was higher.

Spooner is called to the scene of the apparent suicide of a Dr. Alfred Laning whom also happens to be the Dr. that saved his life. When he arrives at the scene he is met by a hologram of Dr. Laning that is pre-programmed.

Spooner talks with the hologram of Laning that states "Everything that follows is a result of what you see here." Spooner proceeds to ask a general question "Is there something you want to tell me?" To which the hologram responds "I am sorry my responses are limited you must ask the right questions."

Your brain is the same as that hologram. Its responses are limited. How many times have you wanted to create a new result but ask yourself a horrible question? For example, let's say your objective was to improve your relationship. Most people start with questions like these:

- Why is my relationship so bad?
- What is wrong with me?
- What is wrong with him/her?

On the surface these seem like normal questions to ask right? They are if you don't want a better relationship. Your brain will come up with answers to those questions and usually not good ones.

When you ask questions that allow your brain to simply respond it will give you quick responses simply based on your past experiences, your beliefs, your state and give you the safest, quickest answer that it can to avoid pain. Therefore, if you are not in the best of moods when you ask, what is wrong with me? It will respond with "Everything" "You are stupid" etc. If you want better answers you must ask better questions.

The quality of questions you ask will determine how you feel. How you feel will ultimately determine what actions you take.

We can now begin the process to creating the right actions.

Heartset vs Mindset

You hear so much about the importance of your mindset and how it affects success. I do believe that what you focus on creates certain energy. Yes, you must think the thoughts to create them but if there is no emotional connection there is no electricity to power it.

What you feel is more powerful than what you think. Don't believe me? What is the one organ in your body that your brain can not control? Your heart. You are not pronounced dead until your heart stops beating. Why do people stay in toxic relationships? The emotion is stronger than the logic. Anything you put your heart behind there is very little logic can do to stop you.

Shaping the right actions

If you are asking the right questions to get the right answers. You have your heart set on achieving it. The only thing left to do is marry them to your objective. We can then begin taking the right actions.

Life rewards action. You can have the best ideas but here's a truth: Your ideas don't belong to you. You don't own them. If you don't do something with them they will move on to someone else and you will see them living what could've been your life. Someone else will be writing that song, creating that business, helping those people, marrying that person. The only thing you own in life is your actions! If you have a great idea at least make the idea pay a toll by taking an action to own it!

Time for us to open up a toll booth and begin collecting. The Right Actions exercise will help with that.

Right Actions Exercise

1. Go back to your Time Line Pages pick the Prioritized Desire that has the shortest time line to accomplish
2. Write the time frame i.e.: 90 days
3. Write the name of one person you really care about that this supports
4. Write what this means for them when you accomplish it
5. Write what this desire means to you
6. Write three **necessary actions** to achieve this desire
7. Repeat with the Second Desire with the next shortest timeline and so on until you have done all four

FORMULA 4 SUCCESS

Priority #1

Timeframe-

Person I care for-

This supports them because-

This is important to me because-

Necessary Actions
   1. _____
      _____
   2. _____
      _____
   3. _____
      _____

RIGHT ACTIONS

Priority #2

Timeframe-

Person I care for-

This supports them because-

This is important to me because-

Necessary Actions
   1. _____
      _____
   2. _____
      _____
   3. _____
      _____

FORMULA 4 SUCCESS

Priority #3

Timeframe-

Person I care for-

This supports them because-

This is important to me because-

Necessary Actions
1. _____
_____
2. _____
_____
3. _____
_____

RIGHT ACTIONS

Priority #4

Timeframe-

Person I care for-

This supports them because-

This is important to me because-

Necessary Actions
1. _____
   _____
2. _____
   _____
3. _____
   _____

CHAPTER FIVE

Consistency

"The secret of success is consistency of purpose."-Benjamin Disraeli

You have worked on the first component of the formula. You understand how to position yourself to take the right action. The right actions are key. You've got to do the right stuff to get what you want. Now how often are you doing the right stuff?

Consistency is the stuff success is made of. Just look at any highly successful person. They are consistently working on their craft. They are constantly looking to improve by practicing, rehearsing, working out doing whatever they can to go even farther.

Take a sprinter for example: Do you think they just show up the day of the race and run? Maybe they run the race once a week before the trials? Absolutely not, they train for hours every day for months. These athlete's workout tirelessly to be able to perform for 9.7-11 seconds. Think about that. Would you trade 800-1000 hours of your life a year to doing the same thing over and over to be the best at running for less than 11 seconds?

Maybe you don't have the want to be able to run like the wind. Perhaps you want to be the best accountant, the best teacher, the best fork lift operator, the best model, the best singer, the best attorney, the best chef, the best manager, the best administrator, the best brick layer, or the best police officer. Whatever it is you want to be the best at how much are you willing to commit to it? How many hours? What kind of effort are you willing to exert?

Doing the right actions is meaningless if you only do them once. To really achieve the life you want to live you have to be consistently doing the right actions. You've got to be committed! We must push ourselves to see what we really can become.

A lot of us are content living below our truest of potential. Not you though. You picked up this book because you are ready to take your life to the next level. In the consistency exercise we take our big leap.

Consistency Exercise

1. Using the Prioritized Desire and your three right actions from priority #1 in the right actions exercise. Write a dedicated amount of time you will devote to each action

2. Write a letter to your present self from your future self. Explaining to them how consistently working at the right actions have affected your family and your lifestyle.

With the letter take your time as you write it. Take at least 20 minutes. Leave and come back to it if necessary. Really envision yourself in the future writing to you now. Who you are because of the decisions that you made.

FORMULA 4 SUCCESS

Priority #1

Necessary Actions

1. _____
   _____
2. _____
   _____
3. _____
   _____

Total Time Commitment-

Open Letter to Yourself

Open Letter to Yourself

CHAPTER SIX

FREQUENCY

"We are what we repeatedly do. Greatness then, is not an act, but a habit"-**Aristotle**

The first thing most successful people have an advantage at that most unsuccessful people don't have is successful habits. The routines that they have for their life as well as the energy they exert to maintain that routine is optimal.

High Achievers usually have the ability to be regimented and focused. Whereas the rest of society is scattered and indecisive. Earlier in the book we were talking about knowing what you want. Now we are talking about how regularly you go after it. In addition to how hard you pursue it.

All human beings are creatures of habit. Knowingly or unknowingly we all have things we do with frequency. As human beings we have things we do that bring us relaxation, happiness, peace, excitement, fun, adventure etc. Ironically the things we do with frequency we usually do with a high level of intent.

We do these actions so often we don't even have to think about them while we do them. These habits become second nature. It's consciously unconscious. These habits are creating our lives. The things you do the most create most of your current life's circumstance.

What things do you do with frequency? What habits do you have that are running your life right now? What does your routine look like?

If your routine includes more hours of entertainment than it does focus on your vision. I can almost say with assurance that you aren't living fully the way you like. If you can tell me more about the latest reality show or the most current movie than you can about your financial future. I would say that money is a challenge for you and will continue to be unless you adjust the things you are doing.

The good news is you can create new habits that support your success. Routines that will enhance your happiness and help you grow.

Frequency Adjustment Exercise

1. Write out your non-success supporting habits. Write out as many as you can think of
2. Beside each habit write how often you do this

3. Using your answers from the Consistency Exercise write out how frequent you can take the time to do the actions (daily, weekly, monthly) your answers should look like this i.e.:

Priority #1
Lose 20lbs
Necessary Actions
- Workout-1hr per day
- Cook dinner and take lunch-48mins per day
- Grocery Shop-1hr per week

Time Commitment-10 hours

Frequency-5 days per week

Non-Success Habits

Non-Success Habits

FREQUENCY

Priority #1

Necessary Actions

1. _____
   _____
2. _____
   _____
3. _____
   _____

Time Commitment-

Frequency-

You are awemazeful! Yes I am taking poetic license. That would be a combination of awesome, amazing, and wonderful. In case you were wondering.

During the Frequency Exercise there was a purpose to you writing out how much time you spend on non-supportive habits. The reason was to prevent you from looking at the supportive habits saying "I don't have time". If you don't have time- make time by taking time away from your non-supportive ones.

We are moving right along! We are almost there to have all the ingredients for the Formula.

CHAPTER SEVEN

PERSERVERANCE

"If you are going through hell, keep going."-
Winston Churchill

Champions are lauded for their ability to win. We admire their skill. We romanticize their stories. We stand in awe of their demeanor. We love some of their charm. Everybody loves a winner. There is something loved more than winning though and that is the ability to overcome adversity.

The perseverance of will is how we rate our champions. The ability to look fear, pain, disappointment in the face and keep coming, far outweighs winning in most people's eyes. Perseverance is the quality that receives praise even in defeat.

In the almost 100 year history of the NFL there has been only one team to finish an entire season undefeated and untied. The 1972 Miami Dolphins won every game of their season to finish 17-0. Yet unless you live in Miami when the conversation of the greatest NFL teams of all time comes up rarely are they even ranked in the top three.

Rocky Marciano is the only heavyweight champion to retire undefeated. He isn't regarded as the greatest heavyweight of all time much less the greatest boxer.

Perseverance trumps perfection time and again. Why is it then that so many of us aim for perfection? Fear. We feel that we'd be too embarrassed if we don't get it right the first time. Truth is heck most of us don't get it right the 2nd 3rd or 4th time either. Your ability to be knocked down and bounce back is a major determining factor in success.

How bad do you want to achieve the desires you wrote earlier in this book? What are you willing to endure? How many no's can you take to get to your yes? Can you stand the laughter and scrutiny of your friends and family?

To accomplish your vision for your life it won't be a smooth trip. You will face numerous rainy days. How you deal with the storms in your life, will determine how far you go in your life! When your will is stronger than your worry you will succeed.

    Time to give your perseverance a workout.

PERSEVERANCE EXERCISE

    a. Write down the names of five people that you respect.
    b. Write your #1 Prioritized Desire
    c. Call the names on your list today! Tell them what your objective is and ask for their support
    d. Write the name of five people you trust
    e. Write you #2 Prioritized Desire
    f. Call the names on your list tomorrow tell them what your

    objective is and ask for their support
g. Write the names of five people you love
h. Write your #3 Prioritized Desire
i. Call the names on your list the day after tomorrow. Tell them what your objective is and ask for their support
j. Write down the name of five people that look up to you
k. Write your #4 Prioritized Desire
l. Call the names on your list on day four tell them what your objective is and ask for their support.

Day One

People I respect

1.

2.

3.

4.

5.

Prioritized Desire-

Day Two

People I trust

1.

2.

3.

4.

5.

Prioritized Desire-

Day Three

People I love

1.

2.

3.

4.

5.

Prioritized Desire-

Day Four

People I respect

1.

2.

3.

4.

5.

Prioritized Desire-

CHAPTER EIGHT

LIMITING BELIEFS

"Courage is not the absence of fear, but rather the assessment that something else is more important."-Franklin D. Roosevelt

"My heart is about to explode." I remember thinking to myself as I prepared to step up to the microphone at my summer job program. Though I had been writing poetry for almost 10 years at that time, I had never shared my work aloud except for with family. I was utterly petrified.

My mouth was dry, my pulse was racing, sweat was spewing down my forehead like I was under a waterfall. My breathing was hastened to the point that I thought I was going to have an asthma attack.

I wasn't afraid of guns but I was most assuredly afraid speaking in front of crowds. What if they hate it? What if I forget the words? What if they laugh when I start? What if they boo when I finish? I don't want to be the laughing stock of the Youth Leadership Institute.

I had millions of thoughts attacking me at the same time. Then came the call to the stage over the rumbling of noisy teenagers. "Coming to the stage to share a poem with you, please welcome Gerald DuBose" it was probably just my imagination but I could have sworn GOD himself hushed the entire auditorium of 300 teenagers. Everything went from chaos to complete silence.

"I changed my mind" I said to one of the program assistants. She looked at me and said nope you don't get to change your mind as she proceeded to push me out on to the stage. "EVERYBODY IS LOOKING AT ME!!!" I'm screaming silently inside my body.

What made it worse was every beautiful girl in the program is in the first four rows looking me dead in my face. I step to the microphone hands quivering with nervousness.

This was a giant step for a shy kid of 17. I grab the mic and search the crowd for my trainer who had encouraged this madness. He looks at me smiles as he mouths "Do it G". I steady myself close my eyes and go into a three minute trance speaking about dreams. When I snap back to reality there are 300 people on their feet applauding. I put the mic back then quickly exited the stage.

An unforgettable experience to say the least. There are numerous accounts for us all where the fear, doubt and insecurity creep in making us want to hide from the world. Embarrassment adds its spice in to make a recipe for stagnation.

Fear is a three headed Cerberus that hunts us our entire life. Waiting to strike and stifle our growth. What do you do when you feel inadequate? How do we get leverage on our insecurities?

First I believe it's important to separate danger from fear. Fear is future based possibility of danger. Danger is a threat of harm or death. One is based on the possibility of the other. Fear isn't real however danger is very real.

Fear only does one of two things it either paralyzes or propels. The only way to overcome fear is to have a **desire** that is stronger than your *fear*. It must be so important that fear can't freeze you. You might be afraid but you do it anyway. You might be unsure but you do it anyway.

Just like when I had to speak in front of that room I was mortified. I wanted to run but once I was pushed out there, I did it scared and look at the ultimate results from that one pinch of courage.

If you want to overcome your fears go attack them with the passion of your desires.

For the next exercise we are going to give you some power to fight back against those nagging negative beliefs.

Negative Belief Defeating Exercise

1. Write down five reasons that your desires are important. Your reasons must be powerful and specific. For example: *I must earn $3,000 in the next month so that I can assist my sister that is sick.*
2. Write down five powerful self-confidence boosting affirmations. Each one must begin with I am. For Example: *I am brilliant*

Desires Importance

Affirmations

Now that you are done with the exercises. I would recommend that you definitely get some index cards and copy the answers from both the Desire's Importance and the Affirmations. Make at least five copies of each so that you can have one for different places. Place them on your mirror, in the car, in your bag, on your refrigerator, on your desk at work etc. Put them places that they will be consistently in your sight or within your reach.

The index cards will help you combat the limiting beliefs when they arise. This is a battle for your life arm yourself properly!

CHAPTER NINE

THE FORMULA 4 SUCCESS

"It is better to have minor success doing what you love than to have the huge success of doing nothing about it"-**Gerald DuBose**

Baking a cake requires having all the ingredients. After you have assembled all the ingredients you then need to follow the recipe to create the cake you want. As they say baking is a science.

Science is very exacting. It's founded on very precise formulas to be able to prove a theory that produces a predictive result. Science is not meant to be abstract or interpretive. The very nature of science is to be definitive.

Over these last eight chapters we have done a lot of work. Compiled a lot of useful information. If you have done every one of the previous exercises, you have created life changing perspectives, beliefs and habits. How do you take those to make the secret sauce called success?

What brings it all together is a simple little four step formula I've come up with. I've done several use case studies and tested it extensively myself. This is to my best understanding what I've found to be the *Formula 4 Success.*

I can only speak from my experience and study in the science of achievement. These are the things that

I have found to be most efficient in creating success in life. The formula is as follows: Right actions plus consistency times frequency divided by perseverance minus limiting beliefs equals success. In equation:

(RA+C) F/P-LB=S

You now have the *Formula 4 Success.* You have the science behind achieving. This simple little formula can help you achieve anything you want.

How does this work for you? Let's walk through the formula step by step to better understand how it works. To help you create the success you seek in your life.

FORMULA 4 SUCCESS

Step One (RA + C)

Right actions plus Consistency

Taking action is paramount, just make sure they are the right actions that take you toward your prioritized desires and not in the opposite direction. The number of right actions you take is crucial. This is a formula after all. You will assign numerical value to each part of the equation.

The more right actions you take toward your desire the better the numbers come out. Add to those right actions the consistency of dedicated time. You are well on your way to achieving your life vision.

FORMULA 4 SUCCESS

Step Two (RA +C) F
Multiplied by Frequency

Frequency is used as the multiplier in the equation. The reasoning for that is simple: frequency is the multiplier of effort. Frequency turns the <u>sum</u> of your efforts (RA +C) into the <u>product</u> of your energy.

Let's use working out as an example: If you are bench pressing your sum would come from the number of reps, the amount of weight, your form. The frequency would be your sets and number of days.

Amp up your frequency numbers to increase your probability of success.

FORMULA 4 SUCCESS

Step Three F/P

Frequency divided by Perseverance

Perseverance is the division part of the formula because it is the great divide that separates the successful from the unsuccessful. The capability to endure hardships, failures and setbacks bares a tremendous load on your ability to achieve. This is your <u>quotient.</u>

I can't tell you how many fall short here. They give up too soon. Stand steadfast for your vision. Life is going to happen. Be prepared to take it on the chin and hold your head right back up. Push towards your dreams everyday like your life depends on it because it does.

FORMULA 4 SUCCESS

Step Four P-LB

Perseverance minus Limiting Beliefs

Limiting beliefs are the last component of the formula. They are the subtracting factor because limiting beliefs subtract from our life. You outclassing your limiting beliefs will be the <u>*difference*</u> in achieving anything you want in life. At no point in life will we ever rid ourselves completely of fear, doubt, and insecurities. You can though limit the limiting beliefs by reinforcing the positive beliefs you have about yourself. Limit your limits then watch your life's success soar to limits you couldn't fathom.

You are designed for greatness don't settle for mediocrity.

ACKNOWLEDGEMENTS

I would first and foremost like to thank my family for always encouraging me. None of what I do would be possible if not for your love and support. To my children, you are my motivation for everything I do. My life for yours.

To all my friends that have pushed me, cheered me on, questioned me and supported me in this journey I am humbled to be able to call you my friends.

To my business partners and staff thank you for your belief in me and toleration of me through this process you make me better.

To you the reader I thank you for taking a chance to let me share my thoughts with you. I hope that you find it was time well spent.

RESOURCES

These are some of the books by people that I have learned from. Great tools to add to your library and journey to success. I hope they are a conduit of creative thinking for you as well:

The Art of War- Sun Tzu

5 levels of Leadership- John C Maxwell

The E-Myth- Michael Gerber

Unlimited Power- Tony Robbins

The Art of Seduction- Robert Green

Me in 4 Seasons- John Haynes III

The Millionaire Code- Paul B. Farrell

Multiple Streams of Income- Robert Allen

Total Money Makeover– Dave Ramsey

Hilda: Tackle Your Inner Naysayer- Coach Jennie

It's Not Over Until You Win- Les Brown

A Course in Miracles- Helen Schucman

Big Magic- Elizabeth Gilbert

Jab Jab Jab Right Hook- Gary Vaynerchuk

Tao Te Ching- Lao Tzu

The Power of Positive Thinking- Dr. Norman Vincent Peale

The 7 Habits of Highly Effective People- Stephen Covey

Leaders Eat Last- Simon Sinek

The Culture Engine- S. Chris Edmonds

Cashflow Quadrant- Robert Kiyosaki

Gung Ho- Ken Blanchard

My Philosophy for Successful Living- Jim Rohn

The 5 Love Languages-Gary Chapman

Leadership Residue- Galen Bingham

ABOUT THE AUTHOR

Gerald DuBose is a gifted visionary on a mission to change how the world perceives beauty. A writer, former athlete, fragrance artist, performer and entrepreneur. He has always seen the world differently than most. A Washington DC native, Gerald's childhood was dedicated to creativity. He began writing poetry at eight-years old, developing a genuine passion for overlooked beauty.

Gerald also known as "The shy guy with a big mouth" has built and advised several multi-million dollar businesses over the last two decades. He has authored 2 other books, in addition to being an impassioned Keynote speaker and activist.

Contact Gerald at
www.thenewwealthorder.com

Social Media Contact: Twitter: @geralddnwo

FB: facebook.com/ gerald.dubose.3

Linked In: Gerald DuBose

YOU ARE A SUCCESS

www.ingramcontent.com/pod-product-compliance
Lightning Source LLC
Chambersburg PA
CBHW071433160426
43195CB00013B/1888